Robert Kirkwood

Illustrated by Edward McLachlan

C000146241

Acknowledgements

We are grateful to the following for permission to reproduce photographs:

BBC Hulton Picture Library, page 10; The Bridgeman Art Library, page 43 *above*; Courtauld Institute of Art, page 41; Mary Evans Picture Library, page 43 *below*; Mansell Collection, page 31.

To my father, mother, Mara, Anna and Fiorenza

Longman Group UK Limited,
Longman House, Burnt Mill, Harlow,
Essex CM20 2JE, England
and Associated Companies throughout the world.

© Longman Group Limited 1988
All rights reserved; no part of this publication may be
reproduced, stored in a retrieval system, or transmitted in any
form or by any means, electronic, mechanical, photocopying,
recording, or otherwise, without either the prior written
permission of the Publishers or a licence permitting restricted
copyright issued by the Copyright Licensing Agency Ltd, 33–
34 Alfred Place, London, WC1E 7DP.

First published 1988

ISBN 0 582 20311 2

Set in 12/15 point Helvetica

Produced by Longman Group (FE) Ltd
Printed in Hong Kong

Contents

Introduction

LOOKING FOR HAPPINESS shares the same basic aims as the first book in the series, **LOOKING FOR GOD**. These aims are:

a) to move away from the information-orientation of Religious Studies;
b) to give secondary school pupils a simple taste of the PHILOSOPHY OF RELIGION;
c) to meet some of the needs of MIXED-ABILITY TEACHING.

LOOKING FOR HAPPINESS has the additional aim of trying to focus on 'the religious quest' that different religions encourage us to make. This is attempted by showing what religious people claim is the relationship between this 'quest' and our own capacity for 'happiness'.

The term 'happiness' of course needs qualifying for, as it stands, it may be seen to suggest that the aim of religion is to create a permanent smile on our faces. It should, therefore, be made clear to pupils that the word HAPPINESS in the title is not being used in this frivolous sense but rather being used to suggest a far deeper state of being that includes such things as JOY, PEACE, CONTENTMENT AND ACCEPTANCE.

Robert Kirkwood

LOOKING FOR HAPPINESS

Like many other people in this world this couple like to spend their two weeks' summer holiday relaxing and having fun next to the edge of the water. Unlike other people, however, they put up their deck chairs and blow up their lilos next to the edge of a puddle.

Of course their friends tell them that they are making a big mistake and that they are trying to be **happy** in the wrong sort of place. They try to explain to them that if they were only prepared to **make a journey** then they would discover a gigantic puddle called the sea where they could really be **happy**.

This couple, however, always ignore the advice of their friends because they can never make up their minds whether or not they are telling them the truth. 'Why take risks then', they say to each other, 'by leaving our little **puddle of happiness** to go on a risky journey in search of a so-called **sea of happiness** that might not exist anyway?' This couple always end up by playing safe and staying put.

WHAT'S THIS GOT TO DO WITH ME ?

Well, religious people say that there are many in this world who suffer from the same sort of illusions as this couple trying to be **happy** next to a puddle.

BUT WE DON'T GO ON HOLIDAYS NEXT TO PUDDLES!

Religious people are not of course trying to say that you do. What they are trying to say is that there are many people like this couple, who are absolutely convinced that their lives couldn't be any **happier**.

Religious people also say that if these sorts of people were only prepared to **make a journey** then they too, like this couple, would discover a greater and deeper **happiness** that would make their own happiness seem like a puddle.

Religious people of course are not talking about **MAKING A JOURNEY** on a bus or a train to the seaside. They are, rather, talking about a **SPIRITUAL INWARD JOURNEY** that takes place inside yourself to find what they often call your **TRUE IDENTITY**. 'When you discover this,' say religious people, 'then you will also discover what real **HAPPINESS** is all about.'

1 If you try to decide whether people are **sad** or **happy** by simply looking at their faces then you can often be mistaken. On the **outside** for example they may be **laughing** but on the **inside** they may be silently **crying**. Draw two pictures (on the same piece of paper) to show:
   (a) How others see me on the outside
   (b) How I see myself on the inside

2 Religious people believe that there are many in this world who are like the couple (in this chapter) on holiday next to a puddle.
Explain what they mean.

LOOKING INWARDS

Religious people often try to answer these sorts of questions by telling a variety of different stories which they believe will help to explain what they mean by **MAKING A JOURNEY** to **FIND YOUR TRUE IDENTITY**.

The Hindus, for example, tell the story of a lion cub whose mother died shortly after it was born. The cub then found herself completely alone in the jungle, without the faintest idea who she was and what she ought to be doing. She spent the first few days of her life wandering around the jungle in a state of total confusion.

Her wanderings eventually brought her to the very edge of the jungle where she saw a flock of sheep grazing in a field. These sheep were in fact the first animals the cub had come across and she was of course delighted to see that she wasn't the only creature wandering around in the grass. This chance meeting, however, simply added to the cub's confusion because she began to **identify** herself with the sheep. She ran in amongst them, joined the flock and took on their **identity**.

The cub spent the next few months doing all the sorts of things that sheep are supposed to do in order to lead a **happy** life. In spite of an enormous effort, however, the cub was not very happy at all.

Hanging around in fields, for example, seemed to make the other sheep deliriously happy but it left her feeling totally bored and dissatisfied.

Leaping around in springtime didn't do anything for her either.

And eating grass all day, while it seemed to satisfy the others, simply left her with a deep inner hunger and a withered looking body.

The cub began to feel then that there was something deeply wrong with her way of life. She seemed to sense that something very important was missing and that if she could only find it then she too might also be **happy**. She had no idea however where to start looking, so she decided, like the couple next to the puddle, to play safe by staying put.

The cub, however, did not spend many more months with the **mistaken identity** of a sheep, for one day while grazing in its field she bumped into a full grown lion.

This lion, says the Hindu tale, immediately took pity on the cub's hungry looking body. It seized the cub then by the neck, took her **on a journey** into the jungle and plunged her head into the warm body of a dead deer.

The cub at this moment, says the story, **FOUND HER TRUE IDENTITY**. The taste of warm blood and fresh meat at once made it clear to her **who she was** and **what it was** that she must eat in order to be **HAPPY** and satisfied.

Hindus of course tell this story because they believe, along with JEWS, MUSLIMS, CHRISTIANS and BUDDHISTS, that many human beings in this world are not as **happy** as they could be because they have the same sort of problems as this lion cub.

8

WHAT'S THAT SUPPOSED TO MEAN?

Well, religious people would firstly say that there are many people around who, like this lion cub, have no real idea **who they are** and **what they must therefore do** in order to be **happy**.

They would secondly say that many people, like this lion cub, take on **false identities** and so end up trying to find **happiness** in the wrong ways.

And finally they would say that these sorts of people, like this cub again, must **go on a journey** to discover their **true identity** before they can understand what they must do in order to be truly **happy**.

WHAT SPIRITUAL JOURNEY SHOULD I BE TAKING AND WHAT TRUE IDENTITY SHOULD I BE LOOKING FOR?

Different religions talk about this **spiritual journey** and our **true identity** in different sorts of ways. It is difficult then to answer these questions in a way that will satisfy all religious people. This book, however, will try to give some sort of an answer to these questions by concentrating on the religions of **BUDDHISM** and **CHRISTIANITY**.

It will be looking at what each of these religions says about this **SPIRITUAL JOURNEY** and our **REAL IDENTITY** and therefore how each of them tries to give human beings a taste of a **happier** and more satisfying way of life.

1 This chapter has suggested that many people are not as **happy** as they could be because they have the same problems as this lion cub. Explain.

2 The cub tried to be **happy** by eating grass but the grass could never satisfy her. Make a list of all those things in this world which others say will make you **happy** but which in your experience don't.

3 The cub ate grass because she *tried* to convince herself that she was a sheep. Do you ever pretend to be what you're not and so end up behaving in ways which you later regret?

Answer this question in either a montage, picture or poem.

THE INWARD JOURNEY OF BUDDHISM

Buddhism is a religion that started in northern India about two thousand five hundred years ago. It is now the faith and way of life of many millions of people throughout the world but especially within the continent of Asia in countries like China, Korea, Japan, Tibet, Vietnam, Sri Lanka, Burma, Thailand, Cambodia and Laos. Below is a statue of the man who started this religion. His name was Siddhartha Gautama. If you look at the picture very carefully you will notice that he has a **THIRD EYE** (two eyes look outwards while the third is a symbol of the need to look inwards). Siddhartha has been given this symbolic third eye because he realised from a very early age that to be **happy** in this world you must get rid of your **false** identity and spend your time on an **inward journey** looking for what is **REAL**. Siddhartha was a man who did exactly this and after many years of inward searching he found what he understood to be **REAL.** That's why people call Siddhartha Gautama **THE BUDDHA.** 'Buddha' means **THE ENLIGHTENED ONE** or the one who achieved understanding.

Siddhartha Gautama was born about two thousand five hundred years ago in a small northern Indian kingdom on the southern borders of the Himalayas which today is called Nepal. His parents were aristocrats and so like most children of the aristocracy Siddhartha's life was very cushy.

He lived in a palace, wore all the right sorts of clothes, ate the best types of food and was able to afford whatever he wanted to buy.

He was also waited on hand and foot. Servants made his bed in the morning, tidied up his room, did all of the shopping, made and served his meals, washed his clothes and even drove him around in his own personal chariot.

He didn't even have to worry about meeting the right girl because when Siddhartha was 19 his father arranged his marriage to a beautiful princess who after some time gave birth to a son.

Siddhartha Gautama then had everything that many people think could make them happy. He didn't need to work, he had a chauffeur, a cook and cleaners, a beautiful wife and child, no money problems and a house with a garden.

Siddhartha however, in spite of his luxurious way of life, wasn't very happy at all. He wasn't very happy because he had begun to think during his more serious moments that life in this world, whether you had money or not, was

nothing more than a very short, painful and sad **JOURNEY TOWARDS OLD AGE, SICKNESS AND DEATH**.

Siddhartha then found it difficult to understand why so many of his friends either expected him to be happy or spent so much time expecting to be happy themselves. 'How can you think that happiness is possible', he asked them, 'when you all know that one day in the future you and all you love will be totally extinguished by death?'

His friends didn't like to be reminded of **death**. When he asked them these sorts of questions they told him not to be so morbid, to cheer up, to forget about the future, to live for the moment and to simply enjoy himself while he could.

Siddhartha, however, found it difficult to take their advice. He just couldn't forget about the tragic side of life or ignore the **INNER EMPTINESS** he felt each time he thought about **death**.

His friends again advised him to fill up this **inner emptiness** with **parties, possessions, buying clothes, making money** and by generally concentrating on having a good time.

But Siddhartha knew that if he tried to do this he would be no better off than the lion cub who tried to be **happy** by filling her **empty stomach** with grass.

He decided that their advice wasn't worth taking and that he might just as well be honestly **sad** as dishonestly **happy**.

---

1 Siddhartha Gautama had everything that money could buy and yet he was extremely **sad**. Explain why.

2 Siddhartha's friends told him 'not to be so morbid, to cheer up, to forget about the future, to live for the moment and to simply enjoy himself while he could'. Why did Siddhartha refuse to take their advice?

3   Time the jailer drags me relentlessly along, however much I kick and struggle against it. His road leads always in one direction – to age and death. . .
      I can even picture my old age. Perhaps I will sit in a chair all day long, unable to feed and clothe myself. Then I will know that my life is nearly over. . .
      And then what? . . . In view of my certain death, what is the meaning of my life?

Existentialism: The Philosophy of Despair and the Quest for Hope by C Stephen Evans

Many people would answer this question by saying that there is no *meaning to life* – that life is simply a sad journey to the grave interrupted by brief moments of happiness.

How would you answer this writer's question? Give reasons for your answer.

4 The sayings of the Buddha
The world is on fire!
And are you laughing?
You are deep in the dark.
Will you not ask for light?

For behold your body –

. . . .

How frail it is!
Frail and pestilent,
It sickens, festers and dies.
Like every living thing
In the end it sickens and dies.

. . . .

And are you laughing?

You are a house of bones,
Flesh and blood for plaster.
Pride lives in you,
And hypocrisy, decay and death.

. . . .

from *The Dhammapada* (published by Wildwood House)

What do you think the Buddha means when he says:
The world is on fire! And are you laughing?

SIDDHARTHA SEES THE NEED TO JOURNEY INWARDS

Siddhartha Gautama as a young man had concluded that life in this world was a very tragic experience. As he grew older however and he began to think more deeply about life, his thoughts began to move in a new direction.

The change began when he saw walking towards him a man who looked like no other man he had ever seen before. This man's head was shaved, he wore a simple yellow robe, carried no money, obviously ate little and appeared to have no possessions whatsoever. Siddhartha's curiosity was immediately aroused and he asked his servant, '**Who is that man?**'

'That man', explained the servant, 'is a holy man. He has decided that he has wasted many years of his life trying to be happy in the wrong ways. He has also decided that he will only find **happiness** if he gets rid of what is **false** about himself and finds what is **REAL**. So he has left his home and possessions to concentrate on this search.'

'But why should finding what is **REAL** make him **happy**?' asked Siddhartha. 'What possible difference could this make to his life, for whether he finds it or not, he will still have to face the awful misery of death?'

'This man', explained the servant, 'believes that nothing can destroy what is **REAL**. He believes that all those who find it will lose all fear of **old age**, **sickness** and **death**.'

This idea was new to Siddhartha. It was also an idea that filled him with hope, for, unlike the ideas of his friends, it spoke of a **HAPPINESS** that could overcome the sufferings of the world. Siddhartha thought a great deal about what had

been said and eventually, after many more questions and many more months of thinking, he made an important decision. He too would leave his home, his family and his possessions. He too, like this holy man, would try to get rid of what was **false** about himself and would spend every moment of his life on an **INWARD JOURNEY** to find **REALITY**.

SIDDHARTHA BEGINS THE INWARD JOURNEY

Siddhartha, when he was only in his twenties, left his princely way of life and set out to lead the life of a poor wandering pilgrim.

At the beginning he looked to others for guidance because he had no real idea how he should start this **inward journey** or how he would recognise what was **false** about himself and what was **REAL**.

He went to other pilgrims all of whom lived in the surrounding forests and caves and he spent the first six years of his new way of life asking them questions and listening to their replies.

These pilgrims, however, simply confused Siddhartha for they all seemed to be either saying different things to him or giving him advice that just didn't seem to make sense.

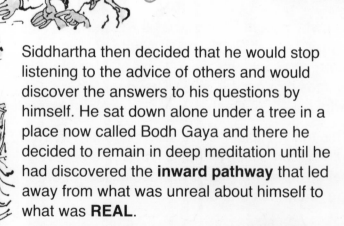

Siddhartha then decided that he would stop listening to the advice of others and would discover the answers to his questions by himself. He sat down alone under a tree in a place now called Bodh Gaya and there he decided to remain in deep meditation until he had discovered the **inward pathway** that led away from what was unreal about himself to what was **REAL**.

'Though my skin, my nerves and my bones should waste away and my life blood dry,' declared Siddhartha, 'I will not leave this seat until I have attained supreme enlightenment.'

He sat there for many days in deep meditation and finally, during one night in May in 544 BC when the moon was full, his face began to glow with peace and tranquillity. He was now, at the age of 30, Siddhartha Gautama no more but **THE BUDDHA**, the awakened one, for after many years of searching he had finally become **ENLIGHTENED**.

1 What changes occurred to Siddhartha's life after he met the '**holy man**'?

2 What would be your advice to a friend who told you that they were thinking of making the same sort of changes to their lives in order to search for **true happiness**. Give reasons for your advice.

3 The 'holy man' was searching for a **happiness** that was very different to the **happiness** of Siddhartha's friends. Explain the difference.

4 Siddhartha was eventually **ENLIGHTENED**. Enlightened about what?

5 **Research**
Many people in countries like Britain hope to get married, have children, buy a house, have regular holidays and spend their old age surrounded by their family. Try to find out about any **religious people** who have decided on a totally different pattern of life and try to discover the reasons for their decisions. (Perhaps invite such a person to the class to explain.)

THE FOUR NOBLE TRUTHS

Siddhartha Gautama was now **the Buddha** (the enlightened one) because, like the lion cub, he had discovered true happiness by discovering what was **false** about himself and what was **REAL**. Many other pilgrims who had heard of Siddhartha's **enlightenment** now came to *him* for guidance. They wanted to know which **inward journey** he had taken, how they might also journey along it and how they too might therefore become **enlightened**.

The **Buddha's** reply to these questions was always the same. 'Try to understand **FOUR NOBLE TRUTHS** I have discovered about life in this world.' Those who can do this, said the **Buddha**, will be able to discover the **INWARD PATHWAY** which leads to what is **REAL**.

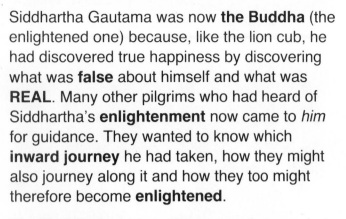

THE FIRST NOBLE TRUTH OF SUFFERING

First of all, said the **Buddha**, you must be absolutely honest about life in this world. You must be willing to face up to the tragic side of living and to admit to yourselves that **old age, sickness** and **death** are a terrible future to face. If you cannot do this, said the **Buddha**, then you will never feel the need to search for a **happiness** that can overcome these tragedies.

THE SECOND NOBLE TRUTH OF THE CAUSE OF SUFFERING

Secondly, said the **Buddha**, you must understand that you suffer unnecessarily in this world because (like the lion cub) you crave and are greedy for things that can never satisfy you. Just as the cub tried to fill up its empty stomach with grass so you try to fill up the emptiness in your lives by craving pleasures that can never satisfy you.

THE THIRD NOBLE TRUTH THAT THERE IS FREEDOM FROM SUFFERING

Thirdly, said the **Buddha**, you will only stop suffering in this world if you stop trying to be **happy** in the wrong ways. This means that you must stop craving and being greedy for those pleasures that can never satisfy you and this is only possible if (like the cub) you get rid of your **FALSE IDENTITY**.

What's that supposed to mean?

Remember, the only reason the lion cub ate grass was because she **falsely identified** herself with a sheep. The **Buddha** then is saying that we suffer from the same sort of delusion because the only reason we crave pleasures that can never make us **happy** is because we are encouraged from our childhood to **falsely identify** with a creature we all call a **SELF**.

We all grow up believing that we are this creature called a **self** and that, explained the **Buddha**, is the cause of all our suffering in this world.

Why should that make us suffer?

Well first of all, said the **Buddha**, when we believe that we are this creature called my**self** this immediately creates unnecessary and painful divisions because we also believe that we each have different **selves** and that everybody should therefore be responsible for looking after their own **self**. This leads to all sorts of **self**ish desires, anger and delusions of grandeur.

And secondly, said the **Buddha**, when we **falsely identify** with the **self** then we naturally grow up believing that our happiness depends upon the well-being and survival of the **self**. This also causes us pain, said the **Buddha**, because we don't know whether the **self** can survive **old age, sickness** and **death**. We usually end up then with the attitude that we should all enjoy our**selves** while we can.

The **Buddha** said, however, that this pain and suffering are totally unnecessary because this creature we call a **self** is not our identity at all. In fact, said the **Buddha**, this creature we call my**self** doesn't even exist. It is simply an illusion that haunts and deceives us and which we must all therefore try to get rid of.

How can anybody believe that MYself or YOURself doesn't exist?

NAGASENA, a follower of the **Buddha**, tried to make clear what the **Buddha** was saying by comparing the **SELF** to a **CHARIOT**.

19

Look at any chariot, said **Nagasena**, and you will notice that it is made up of many different parts.

If you were to separate these parts from each other, you would also notice that each of these parts has a separate name – **WHEEL, AXLE, SHAFT** etc.

But, said **Nagasena**, there is no 'thing' among these parts called a '**CHARIOT**'. In fact the chariot actually disappeared when the different parts were separated because a '**chariot**' is not a 'thing' at all. It is just a word and an idea that we use to describe a number of different objects when they are placed together in a particular order.

Now, said **Nagasena**, think about this 'thing' you call your **self** and you will begin to understand that like the **chariot** it is also made up of many different parts.

If you were now to separate these parts from each other, you would also notice that, like the **chariot** again, each of them has a separate name – **BODY, FEELINGS, INSTINCTS, THOUGHTS** and **UNDERSTANDING**.

There is, however, said **Nagasena**, no actual 'thing' amongst these parts called a **self**. In fact when these different parts are eventually separated by **DEATH**, then the 'thing' you call your **SELF** will actually disappear because, like the **chariot**, it is not a 'thing' at all. It is just a word and an idea we use to describe a number of different parts when they are placed together in a particular order.

Worrying about keeping your**self** alive and satisfied, said **Nagasena**, is a waste of time. The **self** doesn't actually exist and when you understand this then you are ready to take the **inward journey** to find what is **REAL**.

But the **SELF** doesn't exist so you can't keep it alive.

1 The **Buddha** said that if you wish to be **enlightened** then you *must* understand **FOUR NOBLE TRUTHS**. This chapter has given three of them. In your own words explain what they are.

2 The lion cub was unhappy because she **identified** with a sheep. The Buddha said that human beings are unhappy because they also have an **identity-problem**. Explain what he said we **identify** with. Also explain why this causes us to suffer.

3 **Nagasena** tried to make clear what the Buddha was saying by comparing the **self** to a **chariot**. Imagine you are trying to make his ideas clear to a friend by comparing the **self** to a bike or any other modern object of your choice.

4 If you gave up believing that your **self** wasn't real how do you think this would change your attitude to:
   (a) Other people
   (b) Your future
   (c) Death?

5 **The sayings of the Buddha**
See what is.
See what is not.
Follow the true way.
Rise.

from *The Dhammapada*

Explain what you think the Buddha means by these words.

THE FOURTH NOBLE TRUTH OF THE WAY TO BE FREE FROM SUFFERING

It should be clear, said the **Buddha**, that the reason we suffer and are unhappy in this world is because we all **falsely identify** with an illusion called a **self**. If we wish then to escape from our suffering we must get rid of this illusionary **self** and find what is **REAL**.

This is by no means easy, warned the **Buddha**, because this illusion has a strong grip on us but it can be achieved if we are prepared to journey along an **INWARD PATHWAY** that involves **EIGHT STEPS**. Each step helps to extinguish the **self** and to bring us nearer to **REALITY**.

THE EIGHT-STEP PATH

The first step:

Right Understanding

First of all, said the **Buddha**, you should understand the **FOUR NOBLE TRUTHS** about life in this world:

1 That there is a great deal of suffering in this world which we must be prepared to face.
2 That we suffer in this world because we crave pleasures that can never satisfy us.
3 That we can stop our suffering if we stop these cravings.
4 That we can stop these cravings if we get rid of our **false identity** called the **self**, by following an **eight-step path**.

When these **truths** are accepted, said the **Buddha**, you will have a **right understanding** of the problem to overcome.

8 STEPS TO REALITY

The second step:

Right Motive

You must be absolutely certain that you want to escape from the unsatisfactory life that you lead, said the **Buddha**. In other words you must make sure that you are not still living for this creature you call your**self** and that the real **MOTIVE** behind all your thoughts and actions is to get rid of this illusion and to find what is **REAL**.

The third step:

Right Speech

You must also not speak in a way that encourages you to believe that the **self** is real. You must not spend your time boasting, bragging, showing off and generally talking about your**self** as if it were important and real. Neither should you speak to others as if they were in some way inferior to your**self**. You must rather speak at all times, said the **Buddha**, in the understanding that there are no real differences between you and others. You must speak only words that are kind and compassionate.

The fourth step:

Right Action

You should not act in a way that encourages you to believe in the **self**. You must not spend your time **acting** in a way that gives the false impression that the creature you call your**self** is important and real. You must rather **ACT** once again in the understanding that there are no real differences between you and others.

The fifth step:

Right Livelihood

You must not earn your living in a way that encourages you to believe in the **self**. You must not then work in jobs that encourage you to glorify your**self** or that encourage you to treat other people or animals as being of less value than your**self**.

RAT-A-TAT
TAT-A-TAT
TAT-A-TAT
TAT-A-TAT

The sixth step:

Right Effort

If the illusion of the **self** is to be extinguished then the mind must be disciplined. This means making the most enormous **EFFORT** to:

a Get rid of thoughts from your mind that encourage belief in the **self**.

b Prevent such thoughts from ever arising.

c Preserve states of mind that help you to see through the illusion of the **self**.

d Encourage these states of mind to arise.

The seventh step:

Right Mindfulness

This mental discipline can be encouraged by being **mindful** of the body's activities (for example, **BREATHING**), of sensations, feelings, ideas and thoughts. Become aware, said the **Buddha**, of how there is nothing permanent about them. Quietly watch their coming and going until you gradually begin to understand that they have nothing to do with what is **REAL**.

The eighth step:

Right Meditation

Disciplining the mind should also involve **MEDITATION**, said the **Buddha**. (This means sitting quietly alone and concentrating the mind deeply on thoughts like: **a** the qualities displayed in the **Buddha**'s life; **b** the teaching of the **Buddha**; **c** death; **d** universal love.) When this is achieved, said the **Buddha**, together with the previous **seven steps** then the illusion of the **self** will disappear and you will see clearly what is **REAL**, for you will then have attained **NIRVANA**.

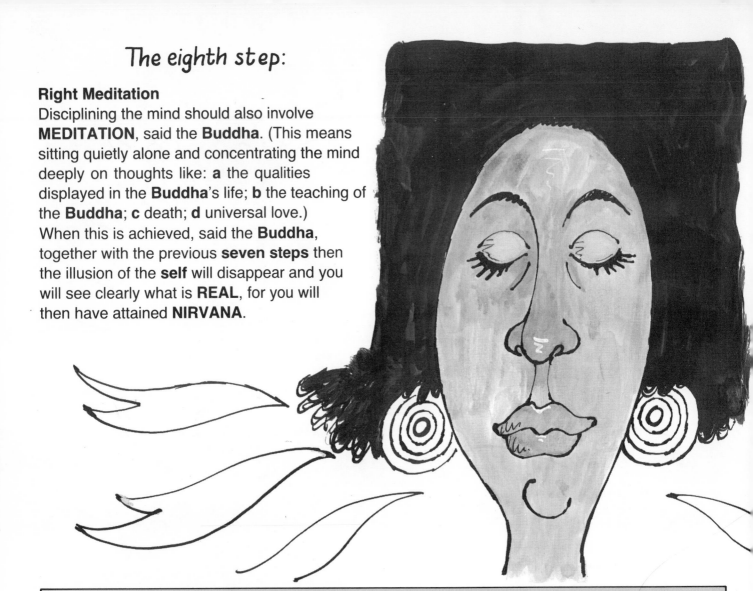

1 The Buddha said that we should try to follow an **INWARD EIGHT-STEP PATH**. Explain why.
2 Draw a picture that will explain these eight steps.
3 **Steps 3, 4, 5** say you must not *speak, act* or *earn your living* in ways that encourage you to believe in the importance and reality of the **self**. Give five examples each, of **speech, action** and **work** that Buddhists would try to avoid.
4 **Research**
   Find out what Buddhists advise you should do in order to aid **meditation**.
5 **The sayings of the Buddha**
   Wakefulness is the way to life.
   The fool sleeps
   As if he were already dead.
   But the master is awake.
   And he lives forever.

   . . . .

   With great perseverance
   He meditates, seeking
   Freedom and happiness.
   from *The Dhammapada*

   Explain what you think the Buddha means when he says:
   (a) The fool sleeps as if he were already dead, but the master is awake and he lives for ever.
   (b) He meditates, seeking freedom and happiness. (Explain what he is trying to be free from.)

WHAT ON EARTH IS NIRVANA?

The word itself can give us some clues because it comes from an old Indian language called Sanskrit and it means '**blown out**'. Think then of candles being **blown out** and you will begin to understand **nirvana**, for **nirvana** is where the illusion of the **self** is **blown out** and where what is **REAL** is clearly seen.

I DON'T UNDERSTAND!

You shouldn't be surprised if you don't understand this idea because nobody finds it easy to grasp. Some people, however, will say that the idea can begin to have some meaning if you use PICTURE-LANGUAGE.

Imagine, for example, standing in the middle of a desert with nothing around you except endless miles of sand.

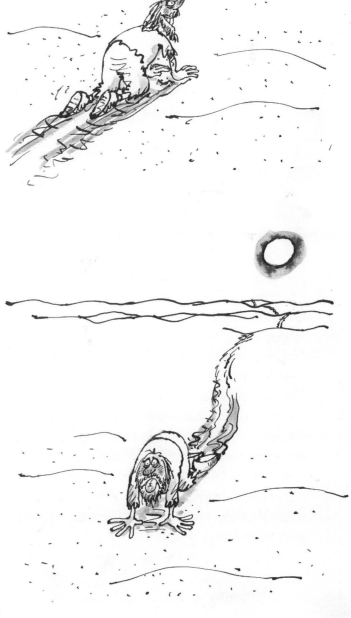

Now imagine seeing in the distance what appears to be an oasis. It catches your eye immediately of course because it is the only thing around you which stands out as being different from the sand.

You walk towards it (because you are thirsty) and after a long and exhausting journey you arrive, only to find that there is no oasis there at all. You discover in fact that what you had seen was simply a large mound of sand that from a distance gave you the **illusion** of being a **real** oasis that was different and separate from the surrounding desert.

The **Buddha** then was saying that the self is like this oasis. It also appears to be **real, separate** and **different** from everything around it. Take the **EIGHT-STEP PATH** however, said the

Buddha, and you will discover (as you discovered when you journeyed towards the oasis) that the **SELF** is also an **ILLUSION** – that it doesn't actually exist and that what is **REAL** is that you have no separate identity from everybody and everything around you. . . . Then you will be like the lion cub, for when you understand that you are one with the universe you will also have found what is **REAL** and what is **REAL HAPPINESS**.

BUT WHY SHOULD UNDERSTANDING I AM ONE WITH THE UNIVERSE MAKE ME HAPPY?

One Buddhist writer has explained it in the following way:

'He who has realised the truth, nirvana, is the happiest being in the world. He is free from all "complexes" and obsessions, the worries and troubles that torment others. His mental health is perfect. He does not repent the past, nor does he brood over the future. He lives fully in the present. Therefore he appreciates and enjoys things in the purest sense without self projections. He is joyful, exultant, enjoying the pure life, his faculties pleased, free from anxiety, serene and peaceful. As he is free from selfish desire, hatred, ignorance, conceit, pride and all such "defilements", he is pure and gentle, full of universal love, compassion, kindness, sympathy, understanding and tolerance. His service to others is of the purest, for he has no thought of self. He gains nothing, accumulates nothing, not even anything spiritual, because he is free from the illusions of the self. . . .'

What the Buddha taught by Walpola Rahula

BUT EVEN IF WE UNDERSTAND WHAT IS REAL, WE'VE STILL GOT TO FACE OLD AGE, SICKNESS AND DEATH, SO WHY SHOULD WE BE HAPPY?

A Buddhist would say that what actually **GROWS OLD, GROWS SICK** and **DIES** is the **BODY** and not what is **REAL**.

Death then is not to be feared by those who attain **NIRVANA** say Buddhists, for it is simply that occasion when the body dies and what is **REAL** remains.

---

1 **Nirvana** means 'blown out'. What do Buddhists believe is 'blown out' when a person reaches **nirvana**?

2 This chapter has tried to explain **nirvana** by talking about **the desert** and an **oasis**. Explain why the oasis is said to be like the **self** and the desert like **nirvana**.

3 Try to think of your own explanation of **nirvana** using your own PICTURE-LANGUAGE. Illustrate your written answer with a picture.

4 **Research**
(a) Find out what Buddhists believe will happen to you after **death** if you don't follow the eight-step path and attain **nirvana**.
To help with your research concentrate on finding out about:
(1) Karma   (2) Reincarnation
(b) Then explain why one important Buddhist symbol is a wheel.

I STILL DON'T KNOW WHAT IS REAL!

Many other people who listened to the **Buddha** while he was alive thought the same sort of thing. They felt that he had told them a great deal about their **false identity** but that he hadn't said very much about what is **REAL**. They complained that simply telling them that this **identity** was in some sense 'shared' just wasn't enough. They asked him to go into greater detail and to give them a real knowledge of what is **REAL**.

The **Buddha**, however, always replied in the same way. 'My task', he said, 'is simply to point out an **eight-step pathway** that will lead you to what is **REAL** but I can't actually tell you what it is because this sort of knowledge is just beyond words.'

WELL, ANYBODY GIVING THAT SORT OF AN ANSWER IS JUST SAYING 'I DON'T KNOW'

Well that's not necessarily the case, because it is possible to have a **KNOWLEDGE** of something for yourself and yet still not be able to give this **knowledge** to another person by using words. Imagine, for example, a person blind from birth asking you to explain to them the colour red.

29

Now you of course have a **knowledge** of this colour yourself but in spite of this you still wouldn't be able to give this **knowledge** to this person by talking about it. The only possible sort of answer that you could give to this blind person is that this sort of **knowledge** is simply beyond words and can only be **KNOWN** through **EXPERIENCE**.

The **Buddha**, then, was saying the same sort of thing. In other words it's impossible to give another person a **KNOWLEDGE** of **REALITY** by simply talking to them about it, because this sort of **knowledge** can only be **known** by those who are **REAL**.

1 What complaints did some make about the **Buddha's** teaching?
2 Make a list of examples of **knowledge** that can't be given to another person by using words but which can only be *known* from personal experience.
3 **The sayings of the Buddha**
   The way is eightfold.
   There are four truths.
   All virtue lies in detachment.
   The master has an open eye.

   This is the only way,
   The only way to the opening of the eye.
   Follow it.
   Outwit desire.

   Follow it to the end of sorrow.

   When I pulled out sorrow's shaft
   I showed you the way.
   It is you who must make the effort.
   The masters only point the way.

   But if you meditate
   And follow the law
   You will free yourself from desire.

   'Everything arises and passes away.'
   When you see this, you are above sorrow.
   This is the shining way.

   'Existence is sorrow.'
   Understand and go beyond sorrow.
   This is the way of brightness.

   'Existence is illusion.'
   Understand, go beyond.
   This is the way of clarity.
   from *The Dhammapada*

   Explain what the Buddha means by:
   (a) Outwit desire.
   (b) Existence is illusion.
   (c) The way is eightfold.
        There are four truths.

THE INWARD JOURNEY OF CHRISTIANITY

Christianity is a religion that started in Israel about two thousand years ago. It is also the faith and way of life of many millions of people throughout the world. Below is an artist's impression of the man called **JESUS** who started this religion. He said (unlike the Buddha) that the reason why so many people are unhappy in this world is not because they are all **identifying** with an **illusion** called a **self** but rather because they are all **identifying** with the **wrong self**. Jesus said then that the only way anybody can find **TRUE HAPPINESS** is '**TO BE BORN AGAIN**' and have created within them a new and **TRUE SELF**.

DR FRANKENSTEIN V. GOD

This is Dr Frankenstein who, like many doctors, spent most of his days patching up bodies that had gone wrong. The work however bored him. 'A person with my ability', he thought, 'shouldn't be wasting his time peering down people's throats and prescribing aspirins. A genius like myself is surely made for better things than this.' He began to think then of changing his dull doctoring for something that would give him the sort of position he deserved.

'Perhaps I could take over God's position,' he thought to himself one day. 'The job's not exactly vacant, I know, but perhaps if I managed to actually **CREATE** human life instead of simply curing it, and make a better job of it in the process, then I might be able to give God the elbow and set myself up as the official **CREATOR** of life.'

The thought of becoming God became increasingly more attractive to Dr Frankenstein. He decided then to give it a go and so locked himself away in a laboratory and concentrated day and night on his plan to make God unemployed by changing himself from an ordinary human **creature** into a life-giving **creator**.

He made fairly rapid progress while working on the Body, for no act of creation was necessary. He simply raided the local graveyard, pinched the best-preserved limbs and sewed them all together to produce his own self-made corpse.

According to **Christianity** we are all **rival creators** because we are all trying to **create** the **person** we all call my**self** inside our own bodies without any help from God. We think that we can make a better job of it than God so (like Dr Frankenstein) we try to make Him unemployed in our own lives. We ignore then God's plans for our**selves** and **create** our own **self** using our own ideas and designs.

The teachings of **Christianity** say, however, that if we continue to ignore God's creative plans and continue to set ourselves up as **rival creators** then (like Dr Frankenstein) we will only succeed in becoming **creators of unhappiness**.

BUT WHY CAN WE ONLY CREATE UNHAPPINESS ?

These teachings say that human beings are only capable of creating (like Dr Frankenstein again) a very bad copy of what a **person ought to be**. In other words we are only capable of creating a **person** that is so confused about itself and life in general that it just doesn't know how to be **happy** in this world.

The message of Jesus then is that we can only be **happy** if we get rid of the person we have created. We must therefore stop **rebelling** against God, said Jesus, and ask him to be our **CREATOR**, for only God can create within us a **REAL HUMAN PERSON** that can be **HAPPY** in this world.

1 Christians would say that many human beings are unhappy in this world because they act like Dr Frankenstein. Explain.
2 Explain what Christians believe we must do if we are ever to be HAPPY.
3 This chapter has shown Dr Frankenstein creating a PERSON in a laboratory independently of God. Try to think of a way of drawing a picture to illustrate how we can create a PERSON inside our own bodies independently of God.
4 **Research**
This chapter has tried to make clear the teachings of Jesus through the story of Dr Frankenstein. In order to make sure you've understood, read John chapter 3, verses 1–9 and try to explain what Jesus meant in verses 3 and 7.

WHY DOESN'T GOD SHOW US THE SORT OF PERSON HE WANTS US TO BE?

Jesus taught that God has already shown us the sort of **person** he would like to create within us. But, according to Jesus, the problem is that we have all been **BLINDED** by our love for our own creation. In other words we are all so much in love with **our**selves that we just don't **see** God's alternative.

I DON'T UNDERSTAND WHAT YOU MEAN!

Look at the football supporters below. They all suffer from a similar sort of blindness. Every Saturday when their team is at home they go and watch the match. Their problem, however, is that they are so **blindly** in love with their own team that they never actually **see** the good play of the opposition.

When opposition players for example go for the ball they never **see** a fair tackle but only one that was a dirty foul.

If an opposition player ever chests the ball down in their own penalty area then they don't **see** good control but always a hand-ball and an obvious penalty.

And if the opposition ever manage to put the ball in the net then once again they don't **see** a well-worked goal but only one that was 'jammy' or offside.

Now these types of supporters are always accusing the referee of being **blind** and frequently advise him to 'get his eyes tested'.

But the truth is that it is they who are suffering from a sort of **BLINDNESS**. The problem is that they are all so much in love with their own team that they are unable to **see** any good football at all coming from the opposition.

Jesus taught that **SELF-MADE PERSONS** all suffer from the same sort of **BLINDNESS**. They are all so much in love with the **person** they have created that they cannot see God's alternative.

The message of Jesus then is that the sort of **person** God wants to create within us is staring us right in the face. But the problem is that we are all so much in love with **our**selves that we all have problems **SEEING** beyond our own noses.

1 Our 'eyes' don't always '**SEE**' what is actually before us. The poem below describes an occasion when people don't '*SEE*' the same things.

> Two men looked through prison bars,
> One saw mud, the other stars.
>
> R L Stevenson

Give reasons why you think these two men, in exactly the same situation, actually saw *different* things.

2 Give your own examples of occasions when people can be *looking* at the same scene and yet *see* different things.

3 Christians believe that we all have problems '**SEEING**', appreciating and understanding the beauty of the **PERSON** God wants us to be. This chapter has suggested that the reason is because we suffer from a sort of 'blindness' very similar to the 'blindness' of *some* football supporters. Explain.

HOW CAN MY BLINDNESS BE CURED?

Many Christians believe that this question can be answered if you look in the New Testament of the Bible (Mark chapter 8, verses 22–25) and read a story about what Jesus did when he met a man who was suffering from **physical** blindness.

The story says that Jesus had just arrived in a small town called Bethsaida when some people brought a man to Jesus and begged him to cure the man of his blindness.

Jesus took the blind man by the hand and led him out of the village and away from the crowds. He then laid his hands on the eyes of the man and asked him whether he could **see** anything.

The man looked up and after rubbing and squinting his eyes for a few minutes said 'Yes, I can **see** people . . . but they look like trees walking about.'

Jesus again placed his hands on the man's eyes. This time when the man looked up his eyesight had completely returned and he was able to say 'Yes, now I can **see** absolutely everything clearly.'

Christians will tell you that if your sort of **BLINDNESS** is to be cured (which is really the blindness of not understanding) then you must behave just like this man who suffered from **physical** blindness.

WHAT'S THAT SUPPOSED TO MEAN ?

Well, first of all the man in the story had to admit that there was something wrong with him before anything could actually be put right. He had to admit that he was **blind** and that he would be **happier** if his eyesight were restored and he could **see** the world that God had made for him to enjoy.

Christians would say that in the same sort of way you too must admit that there is something wrong with the **person** you have created. You must **CONFESS**, they say, that you don't **see** or understand life properly. That you too are **unhappy** with this **BLINDNESS** and that you would be happier if your sight were restored and you could **see** or understand the **person** that God wants you to be and the life he wants you to enjoy.

The blind man in the story also had to admit, say Christians, that he couldn't cure himself. He had to admit that he needed help and that if he were ever to **see** God's world then he needed to **make a journey** to Jesus for his sight to be restored.

Christians would say that in the same way you too must admit that you cannot cure yourself. You must admit, they say, that you need help and that if you are ever to **see** the **person** God wants you to be then you too must **make a journey** to Jesus for your **sight** to be restored.

Christians don't of course mean that you should **MAKE A JOURNEY TO JESUS** in exactly the same way as the blind man. They mean rather that you should 'come to Jesus' through reading about his life and teachings in the Bible.

If you meet Jesus in this way, say Christians, then your sort of blindness can also be cured and you too will have the possibility of **SEEING** the **PERSON** that God wants to create within you and the life he wants you to enjoy.

1 Christians would say that if we are to have our **blindness** cured then we must be prepared to do at least three things. In your own words explain what these are.

2 What do Christians mean when they say 'You must come to Jesus'.

3 **Research**
Read John chapter 9, verses 39–41. Explain what Jesus meant in verses 39 and 41.

WHAT GOOD WILL READING ABOUT JESUS DO ME ?

Well, Christians believe that this man called Jesus of Nazareth is a picture of the **PERSON** that God wants to create within you and also a picture of the **LIFE** he wants you to enjoy.

Christians believe then that if you want to **see** what God wants you to be and the sort of life he wants you to lead you should read the Bible and get to know and understand this man called Jesus.

Does that mean we've all got to grow long hair and walk around in sandals and get crucified ?

No, Christians don't mean this at all. When they say that **JESUS** is a picture of the **PERSON** God wants you to be, they don't mean that you should be a '**Jesus-clone**' but rather that you should be the sort of **person** who can '**love as Jesus loved**'. In other words you should **LOVE GOD** and **LOVE PEOPLE** as Jesus did.

BUT WHY SHOULD WE LOVE LIKE JESUS ?

Christians believe that God wants us '**to love as Jesus loved**' because this sort of '**love**' is for us, like the meat for the lion cub. **CHRIST-LIKE LOVE** is the only thing that can ever truly make us **HAPPY, SATISFY US** and **GIVE OUR LIVES MEANING**.

One Christian writer has expressed the same idea in the following way:

'There is no deluding oneself over this . . . only love wholly satisfies MAN . . . And hence God puts love at the summit, as it were identifying himself with his own Love. Love is man's life, his nourishment, his completion, his ecstasy, his fulfilment. Without love he cannot live; one glance at the opposite is enough to understand what hell is. Hell is the lack of love; here on earth we have proof of this already . . . All the loves that we discover and experience one by one in the course of our existence: food, friendship, sex, culture, goodness, justice, light – are only partial stages preparing, developing and purifying that total, holy love which is the fulfilment of all loves: LOVE OF GOD . . . then we shall understand why we were born, why God has summoned us into existence.'

Summoned by Love by Carlo Carretto

1 Dear Teacher

I am a survivor of a concentration camp. My eyes saw what no man should witness:

Gas chambers built by learned engineers.

Children poisoned by educated physicians.

Infants killed by trained nurses.

Women and babies shot and burned by high school and college graduates.

So, I am suspicious of education.

My request is: help your students become human. Your efforts must never produce learned monsters, skilled psychopaths, educated Eichmanns.

Reading, writing, arithmetic are important only if they serve to make our children more human.

The writer of the letter above believes that school must do more than simply 'educate' pupils. Explain what he believes they should be trying to achieve and why.

2 Many people have different views about what it means to be a **real human being**. In the light of what you've read in this chapter explain what a Christian would say.

3 Explain why a Christian might say that **LOVE** for human beings is like meat for a lion cub.

4 When Christians say that **Jesus loved God** they don't mean that he simply had nice feelings for God but rather that he was willing to be and do whatever God wanted. Read the following passages and explain how *Jesus expressed his love for God in ACTION*.

Luke chapter 2, verses 41–49
Luke chapter 22, verses 39–45
Luke chapter 23, verses 44–46

5 When Christians also say that **Jesus loved people**, once again they don't mean that he simply had nice feelings for them. They rather mean that Jesus was willing to dedicate his life to the service of others. Read the following passages and explain how he expressed his *love to others in action*.

Matthew chapter 15, verses 29–31
Matthew chapter 9, verses 9–12
Mark chapter 10, verses 13–16
John chapter 8, verses 1–11

6 If Jesus were alive today which sort of people do you think he would spend most time with? Give reasons for your answer.

IS HAPPINESS POSSIBLE ?

There are people who believe that it's just not possible to be truly **happy** in a world where each one of us knows that one day we must all face the awful **misery of death**. How can anyone talk of **happiness**, they say, when all that separates us from extinction and total oblivion is a possible seventy years and the thickness of an artery wall?

These sorts of people then find it difficult to believe that **to love like Jesus loved** can ever make your life **happy, satisfied** and **meaningful**. 'Look what happened to Jesus,' they say. 'He was a **person of love** and was no doubt **happy** for a while but like everything else in this world his **love** and his **happiness** were finally extinguished by the irresistible and overwhelming power of **death**.'

Christians, however, do not believe that **death** is an irresistible and overwhelming power. They say that anybody who '**loves like Jesus loved**' cannot be destroyed by **death** and cannot therefore lose the happiness that love can bring. They also point to Jesus as their main reason for saying this.

WHY POINT TO HIM ? HE WAS EXTINGUISHED BY DEATH LIKE EVERYONE ELSE

Well, Christians disagree. They say that when Jesus was executed **it was not Jesus that was destroyed by death but death itself that was destroyed by Jesus** because, according to Christians, after only three days in his grave Jesus actually **rose from the dead**.

WELL, WHAT'S HIS RESURRECTION GOT TO DO WITH ME?

Christians believe that when Jesus **rose from the dead** he was demonstrating to the world that **love** is the most powerful force in the universe and can be destroyed by nothing . . . not even death.

Christians believe that if you have within you the **POWER OF LOVE** then you too, like Jesus, will not remain in your grave but will **RISE FROM THE DEAD** to enjoy your **PERSONAL** existence and happiness for eternity.

1 There are people who believe that life is simply a journey to the grave.
  (a) Explain what Christians believe.
  (b) What are your views?

2 Christians believe that love is the most **POWERFUL FORCE IN THE UNIVERSE** and is even more powerful than **death**. Read I John chapter 4, verses 7–10 and explain why Christians believe that love is so powerful.

3 Read John chapter 19, verse 28 – chapter 20, verse 18. In this passage we read of a woman called **Mary Magdalene** coming to the tomb of Jesus three days after he had been executed.
Explain:

(a) What she found when she arrived.
(b) Who she claimed to have met in the garden.
(c) What you believe about her claim and why.
(d) Why Christians would say that this story demonstrates the **POWER OF LOVE**.

4 Read I Corinthians chapter 13 for a description of a Christian's understanding of **LOVE**. Read it and then write your own description of **LOVE**.

5 Read I Corinthians chapter 15, verses 42–58 and then explain the differences between the Christian belief in **resurrection** and the Buddhist belief in **reincarnation** and **NIRVANA**.

WHERE'S THE PLUG SOCKET?

Christians would say that you've completely misunderstood the way God works if you think that he **creates** in the same sort of way as Dr Frankenstein.

Christians would say that the best way to understand how God creates a **person** within us is not to think of a scientist instantly pumping a **person** into an empty body, but rather to think of the way a good father tries to **create happiness** in the lives of his children.

I DON'T UNDERSTAND

Well, any good father who thinks he understands what will make his children happy will not generally force any of his ideas on his children, for he will also understand that there is no chance of them being **happy** unless they are allowed a certain amount of **freedom to choose**.

Such a father then will not try to **create happiness** in the lives of his children instantly by force and compulsion but slowly and patiently in partnership with what his children want themselves.

Christians believe that God **CREATES** in the same sort of way. He is a **GOOD FATHER**, say Christians, who wants us to be **HAPPY** and to enjoy life fully. He also understands that we must all have within us a '**PERSON WHO LOVES LIKE JESUS LOVED**' if this is ever to be possible. He will not, however, say Christians, create this **person** within us by force. He understands our need to be **FREE** and so tries to create this **person** within us in partnership with what we want ourselves.

Christians believe that God creates not instantly like Dr Frankenstein by forcibly pumping a **person** into an empty body but slowly, like a patient father who struggles with his children, quietly by suggestion and example and who looks forward to the time when they can fully enjoy **THE LIFE** that he enjoys.

1 Explain the differences between the way Christians say God creates a **person** within us and the way the fictitious Dr Frankenstein created a **person**.

2 Read Romans chapter 8, verses 5–17. In this passage the Christian writer called Paul says that there is a battle for control raging within us.
Explain:

(a) Which two forces are battling.
(b) What they are trying to control.
(c) Which force Paul believes should win and why.

3 In the light of what you have studied in this section on Christianity read Ephesians chapter 4, verses 22–24 and in your own words explain what the writer is saying.